BILLY ELLIOT

BILLY ELLIOT
Lee Hall

faber and faber

First published in 2000
by Faber and Faber Limited
3 Queen Square London WC1N 3AU

Typeset by Stylize Digital Artwork
Printed in Finland

Thanks to Amanda Boyle for her assistance in the editorial
preparation of *Billy Elliot* for publication.

Lee Hall is hereby identified as author of this
work in accordance with Section 77 of the Copyright,
Designs and Patents Act 1988

A CIP record for this book
is available from the British Library

ISBN 0–571–20703–0

2 4 6 8 10 9 7 5 3 1

CONTENTS

INTRODUCTION
by Lee Hall

Anyone who was interested in 'the arts' who grew up in the predominantly working-class North East of the Seventies and Eighties couldn't help but be aware of a huge, and seemingly unbridgeable, divide between what was characterised as High and Low Art. 'High Art' was perceived by the majority as desiccated, pretentious, irrelevant bullshit – a symbol of the worst traits of the posher classes. Whilst on the other hand, the demotic and popular pieces of art that spoke to this majority were regularly demeaned as being formally simplistic, or dismissed as sentimentally inclined, as if this were a fault in itself. There were snobs on both sides and both views spoke eloquently of prejudice. However, it seemed to me, there was always something to recommend the plebeian point of view. What did High Art have to say to working-class people? It was their resources that allowed this work to be put on, but it spoke a patrician language that brooked little real conversation with anything of relevance to ordinary people. Whereas the snobbery that dismissed popular forms seemed to be a tautology: popular art was bad simply because it was plebeian. But whenever I looked at High Art it seemed ram-jam full of all the excesses of sentiment and manipulation that made the Low stuff so great. So very early on, I had an inkling that in fact there was no difference between the two at all.

In fact, the accusation of philistinism (on either side) was much more complicated than at first sight. What characterised British culture in the twentieth century was a radical, democratic impulse to free the glories of 'Art' from being a preserve of the privileged. The Proms, the BBC, the WEA, as the most obvious examples, made the crass assumption – that the great unwashed were also unread – mildly preposterous. In fact, the great unwashed were constantly renewing the High Arts and some of the finest practitioners were actually ordinary lads (this was the Seventies) from similar backgrounds to mine. It was the cultural commentators who were predominantly posh, and however well intentioned, were therefore unable to do anything but patronise.

Film culture penetrated my growing up very little. I went to the cinema maybe ten times before I was 25. But I saw much by accident on the telly: *Carry On*, *Kes*, the Ealing comedies and the Woodfall films of the Sixties made a lasting impression. Here was real life. OK, the Sixties social realism seemed ridiculously romantic, but at least the pratfalls and imbroglios of Sid James *et al.* were something approaching *cinéma-verité*. It wasn't until much later, once I had been 'educated', that I realised there was another culture of British film-making, best represented by Bill Douglas and Terence Davies, which had more in common with European cinema than it did with Frank Launder. (Or at least that's what I was told). Until this point in my twenties, I had no idea such a thing as European cinema existed. But suddenly I got it. Here was the class divide – in film. It may as well have been called High Art House. Strangely, the best of the British work in this vein, venerated by critics and institutions such as the BFI, was firmly about class and aspiration yet it was marginalised as inaccessible (primarily, one assumed, by the audiences it represented). Whilst the films themselves adopted the loose narrative techniques of the *nouvelle vague*, and even skirted boredom, no doubt inspired by some East Europeans, they seemed drenched (Davies in particular) in popular culture. Anyway, this was obviously High Art so I quickly became an aficionado.

In the mid-Nineties I spent several years in America and it was there that I started to write. I became quickly amazed at how literate everyone was about film. The arty circles in which I mixed were not just informed about Hollywood or American independent film-making, but had a huge grasp of world cinema in general. People who aspired to make horror movies would quote Tarkovsky as their favourite film-maker (and whilst Tarkovsky may be horrific to sit through, his horrors are of a very different order from *Basket Case 3*). I came to realise that what is deemed the Hollywood narrative tradition was largely developed by European High Art *émigrés*. And whilst much of America's indigenous product is piss-poor by any standards, there seemed to be an acceptance that film-making was just film-making, and it was economics that defined form rather than something inherently 'High' or 'Low' about the art itself. And so it became obvious to me there was no real reason that I should have to emulate the ascetic forms of my heroes in order to address the subject matter that inspired me. I was working on an idea about a ballet dancer in a pit village, which seemed to allow for all kinds of artiness, but if it was about the kid reaching for High Art, why couldn't I strive to find a popular (read 'Low') form for the story? Anyway, I wrote a draft or two with some very helpful input from Tiger Aspect.

I'd been a good friend of Stephen Daldry's since we met in the mid-Eighties at the Crucible Theatre in Sheffield. I asked him to look at an early draft of the screenplay for some friendly advice, and to my amazement he was keen to direct it. I had thought that the subject matter would be too 'drab' for a director with such visual flair and obvious showmanship, but Stephen had spotted a potential in the script that I had been blind to. He had seen the connections to melodrama and musicals, which in my earnestness I had overlooked. And so over a period of six months we worked together on the script.

I suppose that because Stephen comes from the theatre he was actually very used to working with writers rather than in spite of them. Contrary to perceived wisdom, theatre is no less a collaborative medium than film. However, because the money's not as good, directors tend to cajole rather than dictate. I felt the collaboration allowed me the freedom to really push the aspects of popular story-telling precisely because I was working with someone who shared my taste for High Art. Anyway, very soon we ended up with a deeply unfashionable script, a melodrama that almost veers off into 'musicals' territory. If Lars Von Trier had done it (and he has) it would be deemed *avant-garde*, but this is Britain and using forms so beloved by the mass audience one is sailing close to the critical wind, where melodrama is synonymous with sentiment and musicals with escapism. But in the end, who the fuck cares about the critical wind?

What I enjoyed most of all in the collaboration with Stephen is his unstinting lack of fear when it comes to emotion. If you can be 'full on' in the ballet or the opera or in soaps or in a pop song, why can't you deal with emotion in a film? But in the end our intention was not to make a tearjerker or a big splash, but merely to make a miniature about childhood. For me it was fanciful autobiography. Growing up in the North East under Thatcher left the injustices that were perpetrated on hundreds of thousands of people indelibly stamped on my consciousness, and so the film is about growing up in that environment. What seems so strange is that moment in history is so dimmed now it's almost forgotten; so the film for me was an act of remembering. Maybe this is an indulgence, but perhaps a necessary one. What shocked me most was that many of the young people who watched the early cuts of the film didn't even know what a strike was, never mind the details of this particular struggle that did so much to define our current age. Yet, ironically, the fissures in British life are as deep as ever, despite the veneer of 'postmodernism' or the supposed levelling of the Blairite project. This is nothing to do with culture but everything to do with real inequality. Lives continue to be blighted by being denied their full expression.

When I was doing research for the film I came across this quote which seemed to me the most eloquent expression of what I was trying to write about. So I'll let Arthur have the last word:

'I know that we can produce a society where man will cease simply to go to work and have a little leisure, but will release his latent talent and begin to produce music, poetry, writing, sculpture, whole works of art that at the moment are literally lying dormant because as a society we are unable to tap it . . . '   Arthur Scargill, 1984

CAST AND CREW

MAIN CAST

MRS. WILKINSON	Julie Walters
DAD	Gary Lewis
TONY	Jamie Draven
BILLY	Jamie Bell
MICHAEL	Stuart Wells
DEBBIE	Nicola Blackwell
GRANDMA	Jean Heywood
GEORGE WATSON	Mike Elliot
BILLY'S MUM	Janine Birkett
PRINCIPAL	Patrick Malahide
BILLY AGED 25	Adam Cooper

MAIN CREW

Directed by	Stephen Daldry
Produced by	Greg Brenman & Jon Finn
Written by	Lee Hall
Executive Producers	Natascha Wharton
	Charles Brand
	Tessa Ross
	David M Thompson
Choreographer	Peter Darling
Director of Photography	Brian Tufano BSC
Editor	John Wilson
Production Designer	Maria Djurkovic
Costume Designer	Stewart Meacham
Composer	Stephen Warbeck
Casting by	Jina Jay
Line Producer	Tori Parry

Billy Elliot was a Tiger Aspect Pictures Production in association with WT2, presented by Working Title Films and BBC Films in association with the Arts Council of England.

INT. ELLIOT HOUSE. BILLY'S ROOM — DAY

A pair of hands carefully slides a record from its sleeve and puts it on a battered record-player. He lifts the needle, places it on the record and then quickly lifts it off as the record starts, mid-song.

> BILLY
> (*softly*)

Shit!

He places the needle back on the record. The music starts. 'Cosmic Dancer' by Marc Bolan.

> CUT TO:

An empty space on the wall. the music is playing:

'I was a dancer when I was twelve. / I was a dancer when I was twelve . . . '

BILLY's head moves up into our view in extreme slow motion. Billy is bouncing up and down on the bed to the music. He is dancing freely, we feel his joy and the freedom of his movement.

'I was a dancer when I was out. / I was a dancer when I was out . . . '

We gradually PULL OUT to reveal more of him, but still we see his intimate grace as he moves in and out of the frame, seeming to fly like a hummingbird almost frozen in flight.

> MUSIC

'Danced myself right out the womb. / Danced myself right out the womb. / Is it strange to dance so soon . . . '

Billy's hands lift into an almost balletic position. The extreme slowness and close-up is strangely moving juxtaposed to the Marc Bolan song.

INT. ELLIOT HOUSE. KITCHEN — THE SAME

BILLY runs into the kitchen. The music is still playing.

   'Danced myself right out the womb . . . '

Billy takes the eggs off the stove. He puts them in egg cups with slices of bread on a tray.

Music still playing. Billy pushes open the door to Grandma's room with his foot.

INT. ELLIOT HOUSE. GRANDMA'S ROOM — THE SAME

Billy looks at the bed, which is empty.

> BILLY
>
> Ah no!

He drops the tray onto the bed and rushes out.

CUT TO:

EXT. BACK YARD — THE SAME

Over 'Cosmic Dancer', BILLY looks for Grandma. Billy runs through the yard. The camera follows him up the back lane.

CUT TO:

EXT. BACK LANE — THE SAME

Running up the back lane. Past the backs of the terraces and further onto the field at the end of the street.

CUT TO:

EXT. FIELD AT THE END OF THE STREET — THE SAME

BILLY runs into the long grass. To Billy it is almost a jungle. The camera follows him at his own eye-level, running and running as the Marc Bolan track reaches its climax. Through the long grass a figure emerges. Billy gets closer and we realise it is GRANDMA. She is wearing her nightdress and is wandering aimlessly in the field in a daze. Billy, out of breath, reaches her.

Grandma looks at him incredulously as the music comes to an end. Billy looks up at his Grandma sadly. The old woman is close to tears in her confusion.

> BILLY

Grandma. Your eggs.

Billy looks up at Grandma. The camera pulls out. In the distance, at the brow of the hill, we see a police van with policemen pouring out in riot gear. They seem to be dark crows on the horizon, an almost surreal, malevolent presence, quite at odds with the fragility of Billy and Grandma. Billy starts to lead Grandma back to the house.

> CUT TO:

INT. ELLIOT HOUSE. BEDROOM — NIGHT

BILLY is in one bed reading a comic. TONY his brother, 20, is sitting on his bed. He wears headphones and listens to a record. Long pause.

> TONY

Fuck!

Tony turns and looks at Billy.

> TONY

You been playing my records, you little twat?

> BILLY

I never played nowt.

Tony snatches the comic from Billy and smacks him with it.

Ow!

> TONY

Knobhead.

Tony picks up a joint off the record-player and takes a drag.

> BILLY

If Dad knew you smoked that stuff he'd go mental.

> TONY

Look. Fuck off will you.

Tony sits back on his bed and puts his headphones on and turns off the bedside light.

CUT TO:

INT. ELLIOT HOUSE. LIVING ROOM – DAY

BILLY is at the piano picking out the tune to 'COSMIC DANCER' with one finger.

> TONY
> *(off-screen)*
> Here we go, Dad. Come on, man.

GRANDMA is sitting up in her bed.

> Dad.

TONY appears in the open door.

> Ha'way, Dad man, we'll be late. I'm tellin' you, whole friggin' world's gonna be on that picket line this morning.

Tony walks back out of the room.

> You tidied our room? Dad.

DAD enters clutching a coal-scuttle.

> DAD
> There's not much of this coal left.

Tony re-enters.

> TONY
> It's fine, we'll be diggin' it up again next month.

> DAD
> Don't kid yourself.

Tony rushes out, grabbing a stack of placards as he goes.

> TONY
> I'm not waitin' for youse.

Tony walks past Dad.

DAD

Tony. Tony!

TONY
(off-screen)

See you down the picket line, Dad.

Dad turns and looks down. Billy plays the piano.

DAD

Leave it, Billy.

BILLY

Mam would have let us.

Billy carries on playing. We watch his fingers, suddenly the lid snaps down violently.

Dad exits.

DAD
(off-screen)

Your fifty pence is on the fridge.

Billy continues to play the piano. On the piano we see the picture of Mum. Other pictures of Mum and Dad and Mum and Billy.

CUT TO:

EXT. COALMINE – DAY

A group of striking miners are on the picket line.

MINERS

Scab! Scab! Scab! Scab!

CUT TO:

EXT. OUTSIDE THE BOXING HALL – A LITTLE LATER

BILLY is on the steps about to go in, MICHAEL is mooching in the car park ready to go off.

BILLY

Are you sure you're not going to come?

5

MICHAEL

Am I fuck. It's a right load of old bollocks.

BILLY

No it's not.

MICHAEL

It's a load of old shite. Kicking people in. Anyway, I don't know why you bother.

BILLY

I'm good at it.

MICHAEL

Are you shite. Look at your gloves, man. They went out with the ark.

BILLY

Hey. They're me dad's, these.

MICHAEL

Exactly.

CUT TO:

INT. BOXING HALL — DAY

Along the other side of the hall is a row of nervous girls all in tutus ready to do their dancing lessons. GEORGE WATSON addresses the room, as he steps into the ring.

GEORGE

Now, because they're using downstairs as a soup kitchen for the striking miners, I'm going to let Mrs. Wilkinson use the bottom end of the boxing hall for her ballet lessons. So no hanky-panky. Understood?

BILLY is looking at the girls at the side of the room. His DAD, Jackie Elliot, sits to one side watching young Billy with nervous concentration.

GEORGE

Elliot, you're late. Get changed and get in here.

Billy goes over to the ring and climbs in. He looks over at GREAVES. Greaves is a fat lad a good few inches taller than Billy.

GEORGE

Right then, lads. Now give it all you got. Round one.

Billy comes tentatively out of his corner. There is a determination in his face but his punches just don't seem to land. He gets whacked.

GEORGE

Well don't just stand there, Elliot.

George lets them spar again. Billy dances around. He appears to be enjoying the dancing around more than the boxing as he bounces around indiscriminately.

GEORGE

Ah, no, not again. This is man-to-man combat, not a bloody tea dance.

George looks over to Dad who shakes his head.

What are you doing, man? Hit him!

Billy sees one of the ballet girls and smiles.

Greavesy, he's just pissin' about. Now get stuck in and give him a belt. He's like a fanny in a fit.

DAD
(*off-screen*)

Billy, hit him!

We see a huge glove coming straight towards Billy's face. Bang.

Billy is flat out on the ground.

GEORGE

Jesus Christ, Billy Elliot, you're a disgrace to them gloves, your father and the traditions of this boxing hall. You owe us fifty pence.

He turns and looks at MR BRAITHWAITE, the pianist.

How! Liberace will you give it a rest?

CUT TO:

INT. BOXING HALL – DAY

BILLY is trying to hit the punch-bag, GEORGE supervising.

You're not going 'til you do it properly.

Billy starts swinging wildly at the bag in his anger. Music is playing from the dance class which is in full swing at the end of the hall, obscured by the boxing ring. He calms down and tries to hit the bag properly. George throws Billy the keys, amazingly Billy catches them in his gloves.

GEORGE

Give these to Mrs Wilkinson when you've finished. I'll see you next week.

Billy uses the rhythm of the music to hit the bag effectively. Making it a little 'dance' allows him to achieve his goal.

MRS. WILKINSON
(*off-screen*)

Okay, girls, left hand on the barre. Thank you, Mr Braithwaite. And . . . pretty arms. Bottoms in. And where are you looking, Susan? Lift. Feel the music. Feel it.

Billy leans on the punch-bag and sways with it.

In time, Debbie, please. And one, and two, and three, and four and five, six, seven, eight.

Billy continues to move around the punch-bag.

And one, and two, and three, and four, five . . .

Billy punches the bag and then clings to it.

And Hold. Hold it. Support yourselves. Don't look at me, look ahead. Where's your confidence? Come on. And down. Lovely. Oh God. And, Debbie, eyes front. And five, and six, and seven, and stop. For God's sake. Thank you, Mr Braithwaite. Right in the centre girls, please.

Billy stops and creeps around the boxing ring to investigate the ballet class. We see MRS. WILKINSON for the first time. She is moving round the room reciting instructions in a rather world-weary tone.

As she passes the piano-player she nicks the fag from his packet and lights it without missing a beat of her mantra.

Mrs. Wilkinson spots him. Billy opens his mouth, about to say:

BILLY

Miss. Miss, the keys.

As if by sixth sense Mrs. Wilkinson addresses him whilst looking in the opposite direction.

MRS. WILKINSON

Not. Now. Three, four.

Billy is startled.

MRS. WILKINSON

Right, Mr Braithwaite, 'The Sun'll Come Out Tomorrow', fat chance. Ready. And . . . port de bras forward and up.

Billy watches the class with fascination. One girl, DEBBIE turns and stares at him.

DEBBIE

Why don't you join in?

MRS. WILKINSON

Port de bras forward and up.

BILLY
(*to Debbie*)

Nah.

He glances at Debbie and the girls as they continue to dance.

MRS. WILKINSON

Port de bras, forward and up. And hold.

CUT TO:

INT. BOXING HALL – LATER

The girls continue to do their exercises at the barre.

MRS. WILKINSON

And three, and four, and . . .

Debbie, straight leg. Seven, and eight. And one, and two, and three . . .

We see BILLY's legs, still wearing boxing boots, dancing.

MRS. WILKINSON

... and four, and five, boots off!

Mrs. Wilkinson stands on Billy's foot.

Seven and eight.
                    (*to Billy*)
What size are you?

BILLY

Miss, what about the keys?

MRS. WILKINSON
(*off-screen*)

Into the centre.

Billy shakes his foot as the girls turn to go into the centre. He crouches down and unties his boot, as a pair of ballet shoes drop in front of him.

MRS. WILKINSON
(*off-screen*)

Go on, I dare you.

Billy picks them up.

Prepare.

Billy looks at the shoes.

CUT TO:

INT. BOXING HALL — LATER

MRS. WILKINSON walks between the girls whilst clutching a cigarette.

MRS. WILKINSON

And one, and two, and three ... and four, and five, and six, and ...

She draws on her cigarette and walks back.

And eight, and hold.

We see BILLY and DEBBIE, stretching their legs. MRS WILKINSON stops.

Hold it ... Hold it.

She turns and looks at Billy.

Hold it.

Billy's leg begins to shake.

Oh, what have we got here then?

Billy grimaces. Mrs. Wilkinson crouches by his leg. He turns and looks at her.

Heel out. Drop your hip.

He turns and glances down.

Nice . . .

She runs her hand over his toes.

. . . straight leg. Good arch.

She turns his leg out.

Turn that leg out.

She releases her grip.

Mrs. Wilkinson turns, takes the cigarette that she has given to a girl to hold and walks away.

Right, class dismissed. Home time.

Billy turns to look at Mrs. Wilkinson and sees Debbie staring at him.

Debbie, get the 50ps.

CUT TO:

EXT. STREET — LATER

BILLY is walking along and suddenly MRS. WILKINSON's car pulls along-side, matching his pace as he walks along the road. The window comes down and Mrs. Wilkinson looks over as she drives. DEBBIE is in the back.

MRS. WILKINSON
You owe me 50p.

BILLY
I don't.

MRS. WILKINSON
You do. Why don't you bring it along next week.

BILLY
I can't, Miss. I've got to go boxing.

DEBBIE
But you're crap at boxing.

BILLY
No I'm not.

MRS. WILKINSON
Shut up. Thought you enjoyed it.

Please yourself darling.

The window moves up and the car accelerates away.

Billy stops and stands still for a second, staring at the car. Without changing his gaze, he taps the stick on the floor twice, kicks it with his foot and swings it over his shoulder, like a cane. As he does so we hear the music of 'Top Hat, White Tie and Tails'.

SCREEN SHOWING 'TOP HAT, WHITE TIE AND TAILS'
(BLACK AND WHITE)

*It's the Fred Astaire clip from 'Top Hat'. He and twenty other dancers
are dancing with canes.*

DISSOLVE:

EXT. COUNTRY LANE – DAY

*BILLY and GRANDMA walk along the Lane. Billy strides ahead
holding a small bunch of flowers. Grandma dawdles:*

GRANDMA
He was a perfectionist, was Fred Astaire.

BILLY
Was Ginger Rogers a perfectionist?

GRANDMA
We used to watch them. Saturday afternoons at the Palace.
Then I'd take your mum down Oxford Ballrooms in Newcastle.
Marvellous! Mind, they said I could have been a professional.

Grandma stops and stretches her arm.

BILLY
Come on. Grandma, not now.

Billy runs back towards her and pulls her by her arm.

CUT TO:

EXT. GRAVEYARD – LATER

*BILLY is in the graveyard with GRANDMA. They come to MUM's
grave. It is covered in beer cans and it has been defaced by an aerosol spray.*

BILLY
Ah, no.

*He rushes over and starts to clear it up. He is engrossed in clearing
away the cans, then realises Grandma is not with him. He looks round.
He gets up, panicked, but quickly sees her sitting next to
another grave.*

BILLY

Grandma. It's this one here. Grandma! It's over here!

INT. BILLY'S ROOM — NIGHT

BILLY in one bed awake, TONY in the other, almost asleep.

BILLY

Tony. Do you ever think about death?

TONY

Fuck off, will you.

There is a silence.

BILLY

Night, night, then.

EXT. STREET — LATER

BILLY and DEBBIE are walking.

DEBBIE

Plenty of boys do ballet, you know.

BILLY

Do they nick. What boys do ballet?

DEBBIE

Nobody round here, but plenty of men do.

BILLY

Poofs.

DEBBIE

Not necessarily poofs.

As they walk up the street they pass a row of policemen with riot shields. Billy and Debbie walk past them completely oblivious.

BILLY

Who like?

DEBBIE

What about Wayne Sleep? He's not a poof.

BILLY

Oh.

DEBBIE

He's as fit as an athlete.

BILLY

I bet he couldn't beat Daley Thompson.

DEBBIE

Maybes not in a race but in stamina. Why don't you come tomorrow? You could just watch.

BILLY

I can't. Gotta go to boxing, haven't I?

Billy starts to go his own way home.

DEBBIE

Please yourself. See you around then.

BILLY

Aye. See you. Tarra.

INT. ELLIOT HOUSE — EVENING

BILLY plays the piano.

INT. BOXING HALL. CHANGING ROOM — EVENING

Boys hurry out of the cubicles.

> GEORGE
> (*off-screen*)
> Right, lads, look sharp. Everybody out.

BILLY hangs from beneath the cubicle door. He leans up as the boys exit and girls pass wearing tutus. Billy stands up. He is wearing boxing gloves around his neck. He hangs them on a hook and follows the girls.

> MRS. WILKINSON
> (*off-screen*)
> Turn, turn and stop. One, two, three. One, two, three.

INT. BOXING HALL — LATER

BILLY is dancing amongst the girls.

> MRS. WILKINSON
> (*off-screen*)
> Arms are in fifth. One, two, three. One, two, three. Turn, turn and stop.

Billy stops and watches the girls.

> One, two, three. One, two, three. Where are those arms?

MRS. WILKINSON looks at Billy.

> BILLY
> I don't know what to do.

> MRS. WILKINSON
> Follow the others.

Billy starts to dance.

Shut up, Debbie.

Billy turns and watches the girls.

One, two, three. One, two, three. Nice pretty arms. And stop.

CUT TO:

INT. BOXING HALL — LATER

BILLY sits on a bench and pulls on a jumper, as DEBBIE skips. She sits down.

DEBBIE

See, I told you it takes loads of practice.

MRS. WILKINSON walks in.

MRS. WILKINSON

Debbie?

She stops by Billy and leans against the wall.

DEBBIE

What, Mam?

MRS. WILKINSON

What do you call me?

Billy glances at them.

DEBBIE

Miss.

MRS. WILKINSON

Shove off.

Debbie stands and walks off, as Billy picks up his bag.

So, do we get the pleasure of your company next week?

Debbie exits, as Billy packs his belongings.

BILLY

It's just . . . I feel like a right sissy.

MRS. WILKINSON

Well, don't act like one. 50p, please.

She holds out her hand, Billy reaches into his jacket pocket and hands a coin to her.

If you're not coming again, give us your shoes.

Billy hesitates and then turns to her.

BILLY

Nah, you're all right.

MRS. WILKINSON

Right.

CUT TO:

INT. ELLIOT HOUSE – LATER

BILLY sneaks along the landing into his room. He lifts up his mattress to hide his ballet shoes, when DAD appears suddenly. He bears down on him.

DAD

What are you doing going round here like creeping Jesus?

                    BILLY
Nowt.

BILLY lies on top of the bed, hiding the shoes.

                    DAD
Where have you been, anyway? We found your Nana in the
Spar stores.

                    BILLY
Boxing, where do you think?

*Dad looks at him suspiciously. Billy is terrified that he will spot the
ballet shoes.*

                    DAD
What are you doing?

Billy peers under the bed.

                    BILLY
I forgot me gloves.

                    DAD
They were me dad's gloves. You better take better care of
them, okay?

                                        CUT TO:

INT. SCHOOL CLASSROOM – DAY

*BILLY sits at his desk, MICHAEL sits behind him. Billy stares
into space.*

                    TEACHER
                  (*off-screen*)
Copy down that diagram. We only have five minutes left.

*Michael smacks Billy's head with a ruler. Billy turns and looks at him
and slaps his arm.*

                                        CUT TO:

INT. SCHOOL CHANGING ROOM – DAY

*BILLY sits on a bench, MICHAEL stands behind him, Billy pulls on
a shoe as Michael jumps down. Billy stands up and rushes out. As he*

runs past a mirror he turns and stares at his reflection in the mirror. He draws himself up like a dancer and then runs out.

CUT TO:

EXT. THE TUNNEL — MORNING

The LADS run across the fell. BILLY and MICHAEL sneak behind a wall and watch the others pass by.

> MICHAEL

Howway, this way.

Billy and Michael take the short cut.

> MICHAEL

So you go every week?

> BILLY

Yeah.

> MICHAEL

Does your dad know?

> BILLY

Does he fuck? He'd go mental if he found out.

> MICHAEL

Do you get to wear a tutu?

> BILLY

It's only for lasses.

> MICHAEL

Are you any good at it?

> BILLY

Course I am, you divvy. That Debbie says I'm promising.

> MICHAEL

What's that supposed to mean?

> BILLY

I dunno.

> MICHAEL

Do you like Debbie?

                              BILLY
She's all right.

                            MICHAEL
I think she's weird.

                              BILLY
Come on.

                                                        CUT TO:

INT. LIBRARY VAN — DAY

*BILLY goes into the library van. It is empty. The LIBRARIAN, a
tough old bird, peers down at him suspiciously. Billy finds a book
about ballet.*

                            LIBRARIAN
I don't know why you're looking at that. You can't take that
out on a junior ticket.

*Billy looks through the book. Suddenly a man wanders into frame and
pulls his pants down and moons. The Librarian is obviously distracted.
Then all of a sudden a police car chases the guy. Billy hides the book
under his jacket.*

                              BILLY
See you then.

                                                        CUT TO:

INT. BOXING HALL. STAIRWELL — DAY

Girls hurry up the stairs, wearing tutus. BILLY leans in and moves to follow.

                                                        CUT TO:

INT. ELLIOT HOUSE. BATHROOM — ANOTHER DAY

*BILLY stands by the wash-basin. He looks down at the ballet book
and puts it on the shelf.*

                        MRS. WILKINSON
                          (*off-screen*)
Okay, Billy Elliot into the centre.

Billy takes hold of the wash-basin and raises his leg.

Right now, I want you to watch carefully, girls. First, arabesque.

Billy peers at the book.

CUT TO:

INT. BOXING HALL — EVENING

The girls watch BILLY and MRS. WILKINSON.

MRS. WILKINSON
(*softly*)
Drop your shoulders.

Billy moves.

Look forward beyond your fingertips.

CUT TO:

INT. ELLIOT HOUSE. BATHROOM — THE SAME

BILLY leans on the wash-basin and tries to do the dance move, whilst glancing at himself in the mirror.

CUT TO:

INT. BOXING HALL — THE SAME

Ballet class. BILLY is trying to do a pirouette for MRS. WILKINSON.

MRS. WILKINSON
Right, spin it, Mr Braithwaite. Spin it. Come on, spin it.
Now focus. Look at yourself in the mirror.

CUT TO:

INT. BATHROOM — THE SAME

BILLY wears school uniform. He stares at his reflection in the mirror. He spins and accidentally knocks the book from the shelf.

CUT TO:

INT. BOXING HALL — THE SAME

MRS. WILKINSON
Christ Almighty, what was that?

INT. BATHROOM — THE SAME

> DAD
> (*off-screen*)

Oi. What's going on?

> BILLY
> (*under his breath*)

Fuck it.

> (*to Dad)*)

Er, nothing.

CUT TO:

INT. BOXING HALL — THE SAME

BILLY standing in the middle of the room.

> MRS. WILKINSON

Prepare one, and two. Strong position.

They take up their positions.

CUT TO:

INT. BATHROOM — THE SAME

BILLY staring at himself in the mirror. Grandma's false teeth are underneath in a glass.

> MRS. WILKINSON
> (*off-screen*)

Weight on both legs.

CUT TO:

INT. BOXING HALL

BILLY frowns.

> MRS. WILKINSON

And . . .

CUT TO:

INT. BATHROOM — THE SAME

BILLY spins.

MRS. WILKINSON

   . . . pirouette and down.

CUT TO:

INT. BOXING HALL

MRS. WILKINSON tries to catch BILLY as he stumbles.

CUT TO:

INT. BATHROOM — THE SAME

BILLY falls into a full bath.

CUT TO:

INT. BOXING HALL

The girls giggle. BILLY is on the floor.

MRS. WILKINSON

   Up you get.

CUT TO:

INT. BATHROOM — THE SAME

BILLY stands up. He is soaked. He spits out water.

CUT TO:

INT. BOXING HALL

MRS. WILKINSON
(*slowly*)

   Find a place on that bloody wall . . .

CUT TO:

INT. BATHROOM — THE SAME

BILLY looks at his reflection and straightens his soaked shirt.

CUT TO:

INT. BOXING HALL

MRS. WILKINSON stands behind BILLY and points out in front of him.

MRS. WILKINSON

. . . and focus on that spot.

Billy stares in front of him.

Then whip your head round and come back to that spot, prepare.

CUT TO:

INT. BATHROOM — THE SAME

We see BILLY's reflection in the mirror.

MRS. WILKINSON
(*off-screen*)

One, and two, and . . .

Billy breathes deeply and raises his arms.

MRS. WILKINSON
(*voice-over*)

One, and two, and . . .

Billy lowers his arms, moves to turn.

                          BILLY
      Fuck it.

                                                        CUT TO:

INT. BOXING HALL

                     MRS. WILKINSON
                        (*off-screen*)
      Have you got the spot?

                                                        CUT TO:

INT. BATHROOM — THE SAME

BILLY looks at his reflection, as he prepares.

                     MRS. WILKINSON
                        (*voice-over*)
      Prepare.

Billy takes up his position.

                                                        CUT TO:

INT. ELLIOT HOUSE. BEDROOM — EVENING

BILLY stands by the bed and takes up his position.

                     MRS. WILKINSON
                        (*voice-over*)
      Prepare.

                                                        CUT TO:

INT. BILLY'S ROOM — NIGHT

BILLY is lying on his bed.

                          BILLY
                        (*softly*)
      Prepare.

                                                        CUT TO:

INT. BATHROOM — MORNING

BILLY stares at himself in the mirror.

MRS. WILKINSON
(*voice-over*)

Go.

CUT TO:

INT. BOXING HALL — EVENING

BILLY spins.

CUT TO:

INT. BILLY'S ROOM — EVENING

BILLY spins, wearing Tony's headphones.

MRS. WILKINSON
(*voice-over*)

Go.

He wraps the headphone lead around himself.

CUT TO:

INT. DAD'S BEDROOM

MRS. WILKINSON
(*voice-over*)

Go.

BILLY spins and falls.

CUT TO:

INT. BOXING HALL

BILLY stands amongst the girls.

MRS. WILKINSON
(*off-screen*)

Go.

Billy and the girls spin.

Go Billy.

INT. BATHROOM — THE SAME

BILLY spins and completes a double pirouette at massive speed. He finally finds himself looking into the mirror the same as when he started. He smiles.

CUT TO:

INT. BOXING HALL

Having achieved the pirouette BILLY stands there flushed. He looks to MRS. WILKINSON for approval. She simply says:

MRS. WILKINSON
Right, back to the barre.

Billy is crestfallen by her lack of encouragement. Suddenly he realises this is a tacit recognition of his success. He smiles. She winks as he walks away.

MR. BRAITHWAITE walks up to Billy and draws on a cigarette.

MR. BRAITHWAITE
You look like a right wanker to me, son.

CUT TO:

EXT. STREET — EVENING

BILLY dances down the road, with his ballet shoes round his neck. This is intercut with shots of him playing the piano at home.

CUT TO:

EXT. PICKET LINE — NIGHT

There is a huge crowd. The police are pushing and shoving; in amongst the crush GEORGE has a word with DAD. Their concentration is focussed on the immense scrum the picket line has become.

GEORGE
Listen Jackie. If it's the fifty pence a session, you know I can do without it. I don't do it for the money you know.

> DAD
>
> What are you talking about?

> GEORGE
>
> The boxing, man, I haven't seen hide nor hair of young Billy for months. I was gonna say somethin' but I thought it might be embarrassin'.

> DAD
>
> First I knew about it. He's never got the gloves off.

> GEORGE
>
> Well, send him round to my house and I'll sharp knock some sense into him.

A line of policemen restrain the miners as they struggle.

> MINERS
>
> Scab, scab, scab . . .

A coach travels slowly past. The miners throw eggs at the coach window.

CUT TO:

INT. BOXING HALL – EVENING

BILLY dances amongst the girls. MRS. WILKINSON watches.

> MRS. WILKINSON
>
> Step, open and balance, balance . . .

CUT TO:

EXT. COALMINE – DAY

GEORGE and DAD are swept up in the crowd as the police move the miners back.

> MINERS
>
> Scab, scab, scab . . .

CUT TO:

INT. BOXING HALL

MRS. WILKINSON pushes BILLY amongst the girls.

MRS. WILKINSON

Right, let's do it again.

CUT TO:

EXT. COALMINE — DAY

The police push the miners back as they chant.

CUT TO:

INT. BOXING HALL — DAY

MRS. WILKINSON positions BILLY.

MRS. WILKINSON

Open and lift your chest. Right, let's do it again.

MR. BRAITHWAITE sits at the piano and draws on a cigarette.

MRS. WILKINSON
(*off-screen*)

Thank you, Mr Braithwaite.
(*to BILLY*)

Step . . .

CUT TO:

EXT. COALMINE — DAY

MRS. WILKINSON
(*voice-over*)

. . . open, open your arms, do it. Arms.

CUT TO:

INT. BOXING HALL

MRS. WILKINSON

Pay attention.

BILLY turns to MRS. WILKINSON, she pats his arm.

Arms. Like this. All right. Thank you, Mr Braithwaite. Step, really open and powerful. Proud.

Billy dances.

EXT. COALMINE — DAY

The miners push against the police.

INT. BOXING HALL

> MRS. WILKINSON
> You're not concentrating.

> BILLY
> Yes, I am concentrating.

> MRS. WILKINSON
> You're not even trying.

> DEBBIE
> Can we have a go of it, Miss?

> MRS. WILKINSON
> Let's do it again.

INT. SUPERMARKET — DAY

DAD and TONY are doing the shopping.

> DAD
> Listen, have you noticed anything weird about our Billy
> lately?

> TONY
> What you after like, a list?

Across the supermarket they spot GARY POULSON appearing down the aisle with a full shopping trolley. Tony bears down on him and bangs his somewhat empty trolley into Gary's.

> TONY
> Aye, aye.

Gary backs away with his trolley.

> Got enough food there, scab? What are you doing? Eh?

DAD
(*off-screen*)

Scabs eat well, eh?

TONY

You, you're me best mate. First rule of the union, Gary, you never cross a picket line. We're all fucked if you forget that.

Gary shakes his head.

GARY

Fucking hell.

TONY

We're all fucked if you forget that.

CUT TO:

INT. ELLIOT HOUSE. STAIRS – MORNING

BILLY is stuffing his ballet shoes down his trousers. He has his boxing gloves slung as usual over his shoulders.

BILLY

See you, then.

TONY
(*off-screen*)

Wait. Your breakfast's ready.

Billy slams the door. DAD runs out of the downstairs bathroom.

DAD

What the hell's he up to?

CUT TO:

INT. BOXING HALL – LATER

Another exercise. MRS. WILKINSON is concentrating her attention on BILLY. Billy suddenly sees DAD and freezes. His reaction puzzles Mrs. Wilkinson for a second. The music comes to a standstill. Mrs. Wilkinson turns to see DAD.

DAD

You. Out. Now.

I beg your pardon?

The mood has been fractured by Dad's aggressive tone. Everybody stares at Dad. The girls start to giggle. Billy is shitting it. He gives an embarrassed look to Mrs. Wilkinson and starts to walk out, embarrassed.

                    BILLY
Please, Miss . . .
                    (softly)
. . . don't.

Billy exits with Dad. Mrs. Wilkinson stops in her tracks and watches Billy follow Dad out. She is suddenly lost, running through all the possible courses of action. The class are staring at her, startled by Dad's intrusion. She turns and very calmly says:

                    MRS. WILKINSON
All right, which way are we facing?

and carries on with her next exercise as if nothing had happened.

                                        CUT TO:

INT. ELLIOT HOUSE — MORNING

BILLY is sitting at one end of the table. DAD is sitting at the other staring at Billy. GRANDMA is in the middle eating pork pie, savouring it as if it was the most delicious meal in the world. A long staring match, Dad is expecting Billy to apologise.

                    DAD
Ballet.

                    BILLY
What's wrong with ballet?

                    DAD
What's wrong with ballet?

                    BILLY
It's perfectly normal.

DAD

Perfectly normal!

GRANDMA

I used to go to ballet.

BILLY

See.

DAD

Aye, for your Nana. For girls. Not for lads, Billy. Lads do football or boxing or . . . wrestling. Not friggin' ballet.

BILLY

What lads do wrestling?

DAD

Don't start, Billy.

BILLY

I don't see what's wrong with it.

DAD

You know perfectly well what's wrong with it.

BILLY

No, I don't.

DAD

Yes, you do.

BILLY

No, I don't.

DAD

Yes, you bloody well do. Who do you think I am? You know quite nicely.

BILLY

What? What are you trying to say?

DAD

You're asking for a hiding.

BILLY

No, I'm not. Honest.

                          DAD
You are, Billy, Billy!

                          BILLY
It's not just poofs, Dad. Some ballet dancers are as fit as
athletes. What about Wayne Sleep? He was a ballet dancer.

                          DAD
Wayne Sleep?

                          BILLY
Aye?

                          DAD
Listen, son, from now on you can forget about the fucking
ballet. You can forget the fucking boxing as well. I've been
busting my arse for those fifty pences. From now on you'll
stay here and look after your Nana. Got it? Good.

                        GRANDMA
They used to say I should have been a professional dancer.

                          DAD
Will you shut up!

                          BILLY
I hate you. You're a bastard.

                          DAD
Get off! Billy! Billy!

*Dad lunges for Billy. Billy struggles free, runs out the house. We hear
Marc Bolan's 'Children of the Revolution'.*

                                                    CUT TO:

EXT. STREET

BILLY runs up the street.

                                                    CUT TO:

EXT. WASTEGROUND/STREET — EVENING

BILLY kicks a 'Strike Now' poster.

EXT. A STREET OF POSH HOUSES — LATE AFTERNOON

BILLY is walking down the street.

Billy comes to a halt. He looks at a house. He surveys it carefully and tentatively goes up the driveway. We can tell already he is uncomfortable. He passes a big Ford Granada. He reaches the bell and it rings.

CUT TO:

INT./EXT. THE WILKINSON'S HOUSE — DAY

BILLY rings the bell. MRS. WILKINSON answers it.

> MRS. WILKINSON
> Oh, hello.

> BILLY
> Me dad'll kill me if he knows I'm here.

> MRS. WILKINSON
> He's stopped you coming to classes.

> BILLY
> It's not his fault, Miss.

> MRS. WILKINSON
> That's all right with you, is it?

> BILLY
> I suppose so.

> MRS. WILKINSON
> You should stand up to him.

> BILLY
> You don't know what he's like.

> MRS. WILKINSON
> Well, that blows it.

Mrs. Wilkinson goes back into the house.

                              BILLY
Blows what, Miss?

                         MRS. WILKINSON
                              (calls)
Debbie.

                                                    CUT TO:

INT. WILKINSON HOUSE. DINING ROOM — DAY

*DEBBIE and BILLY sit at the dining table which is being laid by
MRS. WILKINSON. MR. WILKINSON is sitting there with a gin
and tonic.*

                         MR. WILKINSON
I've heard a lot about you. Everington's little Gene Kelly, eh.
Your dad work down the pit then?

                              BILLY
Yeah.

                         MR. WILKINSON
Must be hard on the family being out on strike. He is out on
strike isn't he?

                              BILLY
Course.

                         MR. WILKINSON
Shouldn't worry. They won't last long.

Mrs. Wilkinson comes in with some plates and puts them on the table.

                         MRS. WILKINSON
Tom, don't.

She puts the food on the plate.

                         MR. WILKINSON
If they had a ballot they'd be back tomorrow. It's just a few
bloody commies stirring it up. But let's face it, they don't
have a leg to stand on.

                              BILLY
Who doesn't?

                               38

MR. WILKINSON

The miners. Well, it stands to reason, doesn't it? Some pits
are just uneconomical. If it costs more money to pay
everybody to dig the coal out than you get for the coal when
you sell it, what does that tell you?

BILLY

Dunno.

MR. WILKINSON

Well, you wanna think about that don't you, son.

Mrs. Wilkinson enters carrying bowls of food.

MRS. WILKINSON

Tom.

MR. WILKINSON

It it was up to me I'd shut the lot of them down tomorrow.

MRS. WILKINSON

For God's sake.

BILLY

What do you do, Mr. Wilkinson?

DEBBIE

He's been made redundant.

Billy glances at Debbie and smiles.

CUT TO:

INT. WILKINSON HOUSE. DEBBIE'S BEDROOM – LATER

*BILLY and DEBBIE. The bedroom is typically feminine with its pinks
and cuddly toys. Again, Billy seems uncomfortably out of place.*

BILLY

I thought he was gonna hit me or something.

DEBBIE

Don't be daft, he's just under a lot of pressure. That's what
Mam says. I think it's because he drinks too much.

BILLY

Does he drink too much, like?

DEBBIE

He's always pissed. Once he pissed himself.

BILLY

Your dad?

DEBBIE

Cos he's unhappy and that, because they sleep in separate beds.

BILLY

Why do they sleep in separate beds?

DEBBIE

So they can't have sex.

BILLY

Do they not have sex, like?

DEBBIE

Dad did it with this woman from work but they don't think I know. Do you miss your mum?

BILLY

I don't really miss her, as such. It's more like just feeling sad. Specially when I remember her all of a sudden when I'd forgot she was dead and that. What about your mam? Does she not have sex?

DEBBIE

No. She's unfulfilled. That's why she does dancing.

BILLY

She does dancing instead of sex?

Debbie comes closer to Billy. He seems uneasy with her advance.

BILLY

Your family's weird.

DEBBIE

No they're not.

40

BILLY

They are, though. They're mental.

Billy surprises Debbie by hitting her on the head with a pillow. Debbie scrambles for a pillow to hit Billy back but this just presents an opportunity for Billy to bash her a few more times. Debbie retaliates and Billy yelps and jumps back. They both end up on the bed having a pillow fight. Billy hits her. His pillow bursts and feathers scatter everywhere. Debbie screams. Billy is on top of her.

The feathers fly everywhere. Debbie is laughing. The feathers drift down. Billy suddenly notices he is on top of Debbie. There is a sudden moment of sexual tension. They are both very still. Debbie reaches a hand up and touches Billy tenderly on the cheek. She stares at him intently. Billy is very uneasy for a moment.

BILLY

See – you're a nutter, you.

Billy breaks the moment and he is back to being a little boy. He slumps to the other side of the bed and surveys the debris. Debbie is hurt by this moment of rejection, but is trying hard not to show it.

MRS. WILKINSON
(*off-screen*)

Debbie. It's time for Billy to go home. Come on, Billy, I'll drop you off at the corner.

Billy turns and stands.

BILLY

I'll see you, Debbie.

He exits.

CUT TO:

INT. CAR – NIGHT

The car pulls up through a gateway, onto waste ground.

MRS. WILKINSON

Okay then.

BILLY

Miss. What have I blown?

MRS. WILKINSON

This'll sound strange, Billy, but I thought of auditioning for the Royal Ballet School.

BILLY

Aren't you a bit old, Miss?

MRS. WILKINSON

You, Billy. I'm the teacher.

Pause.

They hold auditions in Newcastle.

BILLY

I'd never be good enough. I hardly know owt.

MRS. WILKINSON

Look. They're not interested in how much ballet you know. They teach you that, that's why they're a ballet school. It's how you move, how you express yourself that's important.

BILLY

Express what?

MRS. WILKINSON

I think you're good enough to go for it.

MRS. WILKINSON

But it would mean an awful lot of work.

BILLY

But I'm banned.

MRS. WILKINSON

Maybe I should have a word with him.

BILLY

No, Miss.

MRS. WILKINSON

You know, I could teach you on your own if you want.

BILLY

We couldn't afford it.

MRS. WILKINSON

I'm not doing it for the money.

BILLY

But what about Dad?

MRS. WILKINSON

He doesn't need to know.

BILLY

And what about me boxing and that?

MRS. WILKINSON

For fuck's sake Billy. If you want to piss about with your little mates. That's fine with me.

Silence.

BILLY

Well, all right, don't lose your blob.

MRS. WILKINSON

Blob?

BILLY

So we could do it private, like?

MRS. WILKINSON

Just you and me.

BILLY

Miss, you don't fancy me do you?

MRS. WILKINSON

No, Billy. Funnily enough I don't. Now piss off.

Billy stares at her. Makes his decision, then:

BILLY

Piss off yourself.

Billy turns to get out of the car.

See you Monday then?

Billy closes the door.

CUT TO:

EXT. MICHAEL'S HOUSE — THE SAME

BILLY arrives at MICHAEL's house and knocks at the door. Michael opens the door. He is wearing a dress. Billy is shocked.

MICHAEL
Are you coming in or what?

BILLY
What are you doing?

MICHAEL
Nothing. Just dressing up.

BILLY
Whose dress is that?

Michael goes in.

MICHAEL
Come on.

Billy follows him in.

CUT TO:

INT. MICHAEL'S HOUSE. MAIN BEDROOM — THE SAME

Michael pulls dresses out of his mother's wardrobe.

BILLY
Whose dress is that?

MICHAEL
It's me sister's.

BILLY
Did she give you it?

MICHAEL

She doesn't know. Do you want to try? You could have one of me mam's.

BILLY

No, you're all right.

Billy looks round the room. He looks back to see Michael trying on some lipstick and some blusher.

BILLY

What are you doing that for?

MICHAEL

I'm just trying it on.

BILLY

Christ.

MICHAEL

Come here.

Michael grabs Billy for a moment. Billy squirms.

MICHAEL

Now stay still.

Billy acquiesces. Michael puts on some lipstick.

MICHAEL

There.

BILLY

Won't we get in trouble?

MICHAEL

Don't be stupid. Me dad does it all the time.

BILLY

What, he dresses up in your mam's clothes?

MICHAEL

Only when he thinks everybody's out.

Michael is now fiddling about looking for shoes.

MICHAEL

Have you got a tutu yet?

BILLY

Do you think being a ballet dancer will be better than a miner?

MICHAEL

I don't know.

BILLY

It's just I've got this audition in Newcastle in a couple of weeks.

MICHAEL

What for?

BILLY

For to go to ballet school.

MICHAEL

Ballet school? Is that in Newcastle?

BILLY

London.

MICHAEL

You'd have to move with your Tony and everybody?

BILLY

No. By meself.

MICHAEL

That's a bit steep. Can't you be a ballet dancer here, like?

BILLY

Divvint be stupid.

Pause.

MICHAEL

So when are you going there, then?

BILLY

I don't know. I haven't even got in yet.

                                MICHAEL
What does your dad say?

                                BILLY
Doesn't know.

                                MICHAEL
Fucking hell. Are you not going to tell him?

                                BILLY
Not yet anyway.

                                MICHAEL
He might be quite pleased about it. He could rent your
room out.

                                BILLY
He couldn't. What about our Tony?

Pause.

                                BILLY
What you reckon?

Pause.

                                MICHAEL
I think you shouldn't bother.

                                BILLY
Why not?

                                MICHAEL
I'd miss you.

Pause.

                                BILLY
Fucking hell.

                                                    CUT TO:

INT. BOXING HALL – EVENING

*BILLY comes in rather tentatively in his dancing kit. He looks down
the empty hall into the shadows at the end. MRS. WILKINSON
appears and obviously means business.*

                                 47

MRS. WILKINSON
Brought your things?

BILLY
I don't know if they're right, Miss.

MRS. WILKINSON
If they're special to you, they're right.

BILLY
What are they for?

MRS. WILKINSON
To give us some ideas for a dance. Come on then, let's
see 'em.

*Billy delves into his plastic bag and brings out a Newcastle United
strip, a football, a tape and a letter.*

What's that?

BILLY
It's a letter.

MRS. WILKINSON
I can see it's a letter.

Billy pauses.

BILLY
It's me mam's.

MRS. WILKINSON looks at him.

She wrote it for when I was eighteen. But I opened it. Here.

*He gives the letter to Mrs. Wilkinson. She is not sure whether to open it.
She does so tentatively. She looks at it with trepidation. She reads:*

MRS. WILKINSON
Dear Billy, I know I must seem like a distant memory to
you. Which is probably a good thing. It will have been a long
time. And I will have missed seeing you grow, missed you
crying and laughing and shouting and . . .

BILLY takes over, having memorised the letter.

BILLY

. . . I will have missed telling you off. But please know that I was always there . . .

Mrs. Wilkinson joins him.

BILLY & MRS. WILKINSON

. . . with you all through everything. And I always will be . . .

BILLY

. . . And I am proud to have known you. And I am proud that you were mine. Always be yourself. I love you for ever.

MRS. WILKINSON checks to see if it's the end.

MRS. WILKINSON

Mam.

MRS. WILKINSON

She must have been a very special woman, Billy.

BILLY

No, She was just me mam.

She hands the letter back.

BILLY

And I brought a tape an' all.

MRS. WILKINSON

What is it?

BILLY

'I Love to Boogie'. It's one of our Tony's.

MRS. WILKINSON raises a wry smile.

CUT TO:

They dance. This is intercut with scenes of BILLY's family doing their daily routines whilst moving to the music.

CUT TO:

INT. ELLIOT HOUSE — EVENING

BILLY walks into the kitchen, he puts down his keys and lifts a box of eggs.

BILLY
                                             (*calls*)
Grandma, teatime.

50

INT. ELLIOT HOUSE. BEDROOM — VERY EARLY

TONY gets out of bed early. He tries not to wake BILLY.

> BILLY
>
> Where are you going?

> TONY
>
> Go back to sleep.

> BILLY
>
> It's four o' clock.

INT. KITCHEN — THE SAME

TONY goes into the toolbox which is in the cupboard under the sink. He is rooting through it, he takes out a hammer. He hasn't noticed DAD sitting waiting. Tony looks at Dad.

> DAD
>
> You weren't thinking of taking it with you?

Dad looks at Tony.

> TONY
>
> You just wanna stand round . . . getting the shit kicked out of you, that's your funeral. But some of us are ready to fight back for once. They're already after you, for fuck's sake.

> DAD
>
> You're no good to us in jail.

> TONY
>
> I don't plan on getting caught.

BILLY appears.

> BILLY
>
> What's going on?

> DAD
>
> You get back to bed! Both of you!

TONY

Fuck you.

DAD

Put it down.

TONY

Are you going to stop me?

DAD

I'm warning you.

TONY

You haven't got it in you, man, you're finished. Since Mam died you're nothing but a useless twat! What the fuck are you gonna do about it?

Dad hits Tony in the face. Tony staggers back.

Billy screams in slow motion:

BILLY

Stop it!

Billy stands there terrified. Tony gets up, grabs the hammer. For a moment we think he might use it on Dad, but he puts it into his pocket. Tony is shaken too but he leaves. Dad makes no attempt to stop him. Dad sits down at the table. Billy stares at him.

DAD

What the fuck are you looking at?

MRS. WILKINSON
(off-screen)

You haven't been practising.

CUT TO:

INT. BOXING HALL — LATE AFTERNOON

BILLY is dancing. He is incredibly tense. He is unable to do his combination because he can't relax.

MRS. WILKINSON

Prepare. One, two. And one and two.

BILLY spins and falls on the floor.

52

Get up.

> BILLY

Miss. I can't do it.

> MRS. WILKINSON

That's because you're not concentrating.

> BILLY

Miss, I am concentrating.

> MRS. WILKINSON

You're not even trying.

> BILLY

I am, Miss.

> MRS. WILKINSON

Do it again.

> BILLY

I can't.

> MRS. WILKINSON

You do it again.

Mrs. Wilkinson is at her most tyrannical. Billy is frozen in hopeless indecision, terrified by her. He then builds himself up to a small defiance.

> BILLY

No.

Billy looks at her and runs out.

> MRS. WILKINSON
> (*softly*)

Shit.

CUT TO:

INT. BOXING HALL. CUBICLES — THE SAME

BILLY is crying. MRS. WILKINSON comes up tentatively.

> MRS. WILKINSON

I'm sorry.

BILLY

It's all right for you. It's not you who has to do it.

MRS. WILKINSON

I know.

BILLY

You don't know anything. What do you know in your posh house with your husband that pisses his self. You're the same as everybody else, all you want is to tell me what to do.

MRS. WILKINSON

Now wait a minute.

BILLY

Look, I don't want to do your stupid fuckin' audition. You only want me to do it for your own benefit.

MRS. WILKINSON

Look, Billy . . .

BILLY

Because you're a failure.

MRS. WILKINSON

Don't you dare talk to me like that.

BILLY

You haven't even got a proper dancing school. You're stuck in some crummy school gym. Don't pick on me just cos you've fucked up your life.

Mrs. Wilkinson slaps Billy. She realises what she has done. Billy just stares at her. She is shaken. She reaches out to hug Billy; we don't know whether he will run away. Suddenly he bursts into tears and hugs Mrs. Wilkinson. We see Mrs. Wilkinson is in tears too. Finally, Billy pulls away.

CUT TO:

INT. BOXING HALL — THE SAME

BILLY dances.

CUT TO:

EXT. ROAD — DAY

MRS. WILKINSON's car drives up the road.

> BILLY
> (*voice-over*)
> Can I put a tape on, Miss?

> MRS. WILKINSON
> (*voice-over*)
> Oh, all right, if you must.

CUT TO:

EXT. TRANSPORTER BRIDGE — THE SAME

The car drives onto the bridge.

CUT TO:

INT. PARKED CAR — THE SAME

MRS. WILKINSON is listening to the music as intently as BILLY now. She is smoking a fag, obviously affected by the emotion. The tape runs out.

BILLY

It's cush isn't it.
So is there a story, Miss?

MRS. WILKINSON

Of course. It's about a woman who has been captured by an
evil magician.

BILLY

It sounds crap.

MRS. WILKINSON

And this woman, this beautiful woman is forced to be a swan,
except for a few hours every night when she becomes alive. When
she becomes real again. And then one night she meets this young
prince and he falls in love with her and she realises this is the one
thing that will allow her to become a real woman once more.

BILLY

So then what happens?

MRS. WILKINSON

He promises to marry her and then goes off with somebody
else, of course.

BILLY

So she has to be a swan for good.

WILKINSON

She dies.

BILLY

Cos the prince didn't love her?

MRS. WILKINSON

Come on, it's time to go. It's only a ghost story.

Mrs. Wilkinson starts the engine.

CUT TO:

INT. ELLIOT HOUSE — LATER

*BILLY, dressed in a dressing-gown, clutches a drink. He peers through
the glass-panelled door and slowly slides it open.*

GRANDMA is lying in bed. She sits up quickly.

GRANDMA

No! No. No.

BILLY

It's me.

Pause.

It's Billy.

Billy walks back into the dark kitchen. He opens the fridge and takes out some milk, in the light we see MUM is standing in the kitchen. He drinks from the bottle. Mum speaks. BILLY acts as if this is perfectly natural.

MUM

Oi, little'un . . .

Billy turns round and sees Mum.

MUM

. . . What have I told you about drinking from the bottle?

BILLY

Sorry, Mam.

Billy takes a glass and pours himself some milk. He puts the milk on the top of the fridge.

MUM

Well, put it back.

Billy picks up the bottle and puts it back. He turns round. Mum is gone.

CUT TO:

INT. BOXING HALL — DAY

BILLY and DEBBIE sit on a bench. Debbie sucks a lollipop and glances at Billy.

DEBBIE

When's the audition then?

> BILLY
Tomorrow morning.

Pause.

> DEBBIE
I'll miss you if you go away.

> BILLY
Who do you think's better – Fred Astaire or Ginger Rogers?

Billy bends to pick up his ballet shoes.

> DEBBIE
Billy, do you not fancy us, like?

> BILLY
Dunno, never really thought about it.

> DEBBIE
If you want I'll show you me fanny.

> BILLY
Nah, you're all right.

CUT TO:

EXT. STREETS – DAY

Miners hurry downhill chased by armed police. A miner trips, others gather around him and help him up.

TONY runs through a series of houses, chased by police, spitting at a police van as he goes.

When he reaches the last house he runs out the back door only to be greeted by a large line of riot police. Tony runs back and up a street filled with washing.

BILLY, who has been caught up in the fighting, stands on a wall watching. He sees Tony running up the street, covered in a sheet. He is running towards a group of police.

> BILLY
Tony!

Tony is beaten by the police and trundled into a police van.

INT. ELLIOT HOUSE — EVENING

BILLY sits on the floor clutching the telephone. He glances around as he dials.

CUT TO:

INT. WILKINSON HOUSE — THE SAME

DEBBIE is in the living room. The phone rings; she picks it up.

> BILLY
> (*voice-over*)
> (*on phone*)
Miss? It's about the audition . . .

CUT TO:

INT. ELLIOT HOUSE — THE SAME

BILLY frowns.

> BILLY
Hello?

CUT TO:

INT. WILKINSON HOUSE — THE SAME

DEBBIE puts the phone down.

CUT TO:

INT. ELLIOT HOUSE — THE SAME

BILLY slowly replaces the receiver.

CUT TO:

> COURT USHER
> (*voice-over*)
Right, listings for court four.

CUT TO:

INT. COURTHOUSE WAITING AREA — DAY

> COURT USHER
Tony Elliot. George Brunton.

TONY walks into the courtroom, BILLY follows.

> BILLY
> (*To a POLICEMAN standing at the court door*)
> What's the time?

> POLICEMAN
> It's ten past ten.

CUT TO:

INT. BOXING HALL — THE SAME

MRS. WILKINSON stands in the middle of the boxing ring.

> MRS. WILKINSON
> Oh, Billy!

She turns, picks up her bag and steps between the ropes.

CUT TO:

EXT. STREET — DAY

MRS. WILKINSON walks up the road, glancing at a piece of paper in her hand. She sees a little girl in the street.

> MRS. WILKINSON
> Hello.

A neighbour, SHEILA, leans over a gate.

> SHEILA
> Can I help you?

> MRS. WILKINSON
> Yeah, I was looking for . . .

> SHEILA
> They're out.

> MRS. WILKINSON
> Sorry.

MRS. WILKINSON turns. She sees BILLY, TONY and DAD walking up the road.

BILLY

Please, Miss. Don't.

MRS. WILKINSON

What's going on, Billy?

TONY

Who the fuck are you?

DAD

I think we better go inside.

INT. ELLIOT HOUSE — THE SAME

DAD, BILLY, TONY and MRS. WILKINSON are in the front room. They are all sitting round the table. Tony seems amazed at what he is hearing.

MRS. WILKINSON

I know this might be a bit difficult for you, but today Billy missed an important audition.

Stunned silence. Tony is trying to take all this in.

TONY

Audition!?

MRS. WILKINSON

For the Royal Ballet School.

Dad rubs his face. Silence. No one knows what to say.

TONY

The Royal Ballet.

MRS. WILKINSON

School. Where they teach the Ballet.

Tony is completely gobsmacked. He slowly bursts into hysterical laughter.

TONY

You've got to be joking, though.

MRS. WILKINSON

No, I'm perfectly serious.

Tony looks at Billy.

TONY

Have you any idea what we're going through? . . . and you come round spouting shite. And you . . . fuckin' Ballet. What you trying to do, make him a fuckin' scab for the rest of his life? Look at him. He's only eleven for fuck's sake.

BILLY

You've got to start training from when you're young.

TONY

Shut it. I'm not having any brother of mine running round like a right twat for your gratification.

MRS. WILKINSON

Excuse me, it's not for my gratification.

TONY

And what good's it going to do him? You're not taking him away. He's only a bairn. What about giving him a childhood?

BILLY

But I don't want a childhood; I want to be a ballet dancer.

TONY

And anyway what do you know about it? What qualifications have you got?

MRS. WILKINSON

Look, I haven't come here to defend myself.

TONY

For all we know you could be some fuckin' nutter. Get the fuckin' social on you.

MRS. WILKINSON

I think you should calm yourself down, son.

TONY

Well, you say he can dance. Well, go on, dance, then.

Billy looks in surprise.

TONY

Let's see this fuckin' dancing.

Billy does not move. Tony suddenly grabs him and sticks him on the table.

MRS. WILKINSON

Oh no. No. This is ridiculous.

TONY

Go on then. If you're a fuckin' ballet dancer, then let's be having you.

MRS. WILKINSON

Don't you dare.

Billy is standing on the table in shock.

TONY

What sort of teacher are you? He's got the chance to dance and now you're fuckin' well telling him not to. Dance you little twat. No? So piss off. He's not doing any more fuckin' ballet. And if you go anywhere near him again, I'll smack you one, you middle-class cow.

Whilst Tony and Mrs. Wilkinson battle it out, we see the room from Billy's perspective and he is shut off from the mad argument.

Mrs. Wilkinson's speech is intercut with Billy dancing a dance of anger outside the house.

MRS. WILKINSON

Hang on a minute. You don't know anything about me, you sanctimonious little shit. What are you scared of? That he won't grow up to race whippets or grow leeks or piss his wages up the wall? Listen, I've been with him every night for two months now and you haven't even noticed. So don't lecture me on the British fucking class system, comrade. See you, Billy.

Mrs. Wilkinson turns and leaves.

CUT TO:

EXT. BACK YARD — THE SAME

We see BILLY continue to dance angrily outside. He kicks and stomps all his anger out. He kicks at the wall and leaps up it. He winds down the lane; it is a dance as well as a cathartic fit.

CUT TO:

BILLY tap-dancing wildly up a street. He reaches a brick wall at the end and collapses. We pan back round to see MICHAEL now in winter clothes and the street covered in snow.

MICHAEL

Are you coming or what?

BILLY now also in winter clothes kicks away from the wall and walks towards Michael through the snow.

GEORGE
(voice-over)
(shouts)

Merry Christmas, everybody.

CUT TO:

INT. SOCIAL CLUB — EVENING

A banner says 'Merry Christmas – 9 months. We shall not be moved.'

The club is full of people and there are many children running around. GEORGE is on stage. The crowd begins to chant:

> CROWD
> Here we go, here we go, here we go.

CUT TO:

EXT. BACK YARD — DAY

It is freezing. A layer of snow covers everything. DAD is in the back yard with an axe. He is hacking away at the carcass of the old piano.

Billy is watching.

> BILLY
> Do you think she'll mind?

> DAD
> Shut it, Billy. She's dead.

INT. ELLIOT HOUSE — THE SAME

BILLY puts bits of the piano onto the fire and then joins GRANDMA and DAD at the table. TONY comes through with a chicken. They are all wearing party hats.

> DAD
> Well, Merry Christmas, everybody.

> BILLY
> Merry Christmas.

> GRANDMA
> Merry Christmas.

> TONY
> Merry Christmas.

Suddenly, Billy looks over at Dad we see tears in his eyes. He is sitting upright as if ready to eat dinner, but he just sits staring at the food. We see that he cannot take the strain any more. Billy looks on helplessly.

CUT TO:

EXT. THE STREET — EVENING

BILLY and MICHAEL alone. They are building a snowman.

> BILLY
> A fuckin' great Christmas this has been.

> MICHAEL
> Go on. Have some.

MICHAEL passes BILLY some cider.

> BILLY
> Where did you get it?

> MICHAEL
> Me dad's got loads in the kitchen.

> BILLY
> Won't he notice?

MICHAEL

He never knows how much there is.

BILLY

Tastes of piss.

MICHAEL

You get used to it. Maybes, you could run away or something. You know, join a dancing troop.

BILLY

Don't be so stupid.

MICHAEL

Well, maybe it's all for the best.

BILLY

What do you mean?

MICHAEL

Well, you won't have to go away or nothing.

BILLY

My hands are freezing.

MICHAEL

Givez'em here.

Michael grabs Billy's hands and sticks them down his jumper. They stand very close to each other. The tension is palpable.

BILLY

What are you doing?

MICHAEL

Nothing. Just warming your hands.

BILLY

You're not a poof or owt?

MICHAEL

What gave you that impression?

BILLY

Aren't me hands cold?

> MICHAEL

I quite like it.

Michael can stand it no longer; he kisses Billy. Billy pulls away.

> BILLY

Just cos I like ballet, doesn't mean I'm a poof, you know.

> MICHAEL

You won't tell anybody will you?

Billy smiles.

> BILLY

Come on.

> CUT TO:

INT. BOXING HALL – THE SAME

BILLY and MICHAEL sneak in. They turn the lights on. He plugs in the tape-recorder.

> MICHAEL

It's fucking freezing in here.

> BILLY

Here.

Billy hands Michael a tutu.

> MICHAEL

What's this?

> BILLY

Just put it on.

> CUT TO:

EXT. STREET BELOW – THE SAME

GEORGE and DAD and several blokes are walking home.

> MINER

George. George – there's somebody in the club.

GEORGE
This kangaroo, he's walking away over it, right? And he's called, er, Norman. And then round the corner came this wallaby.

George approaches the hall.

CUT TO:

INT. BOXING HALL — THE SAME

The boys are in the boxing ring. Michael is wearing a tutu.
BILLY demonstrates ballet moves, Michael copies them.

BILLY
Plié, first.

MICHAEL
What's a plié?

BILLY
It's French.

MICHAEL
Why is it French?

BILLY

I dunno. Second. Like a princess. Second, and down. And first. Carry on. Fifth. Shoulders down. Long neck.

MICHAEL

How do I look?

BILLY

Shut up, you poof!

MICHAEL

Fuck off.

GEORGE enters, clutching a bottle and stares at the boys. The boys don't see him.

BILLY

Second and down. And first. Fifth.

CUT TO:

EXT. STREET – LATER

DAD is walking down the street. GEORGE comes running up.

GEORGE

Jackie. Jackie man.

Dad looks at him.

Here.

CUT TO:

INT. BOXING CLUB – THE SAME

BILLY and MICHAEL are messing around. Billy hangs on a rope.

MICHAEL

Give us your hand.

Michael takes Billy's hand and pulls him.

MICHAEL

Dance.

DAD enters.

Billy looks at Dad in surprise, unsure as to what this really means.

70

Michael takes off the tutu.

*Billy starts to dance. He is tentative but as the music rises Billy rises to it.
The dance is a culmination of all the movements we have seen so far.*

Billy stops. Michael claps. Dad walks out.

CUT TO:

EXT. STREET. EVENING.

DAD walks down the road. BILLY follows him.

BILLY

Dad!

DAD

Go home, son.

CUT TO:

EXT. WILKINSON HOUSE — NIGHT

DAD in his donkey jacket trudges through the snow. He sees the Wilkinson's house. He rings on the bell.

CUT TO:

INT. WILKINSON HOUSE — NIGHT

MR. WILKINSON opens the door. On seeing DAD he calls back over his shoulder to Mrs. Wilkinson.

MR. WILKINSON
(*to Mrs. Wilkinson*)
Is this a friend of yours then?

MRS. WILKINSON is slumped on the sofa.

DAD
How much is it gonna cost?

MRS. WILKINSON
And a Happy Christmas to you too.

Mrs Wilkinson shakes her head.

Not as much as you might think. Maybe two grand. But there's a good chance the council's . . .

DAD
Two grand? I was, I was talking about the auditions.

MRS. WILKINSON
Look, if it's just a matter of the trip to London. I'll give you the money for the fare.

DAD
I didn't come here to be patronised.

MRS. WILKINSON
Oh, no one's trying to patronise you. You're being ridiculous.

DAD
Am I?

MRS. WILKINSON
Yes.

DAD
Thanks for everything you've done for Billy. But he is my son, isn't he?

CUT TO:

INT. ELLIOT HOUSE. BILLY'S ROOM — THE SAME

DAD is pissed, he stumbles into Billy's room. TONY is fast asleep. Dad maudlin drunk sits on the bed; he looks at BILLY. Billy is awake. He sits up but doesn't say anything.

EXT. WASTELAND — EARLY MORNING

DAD trudges across waste ground. As he continues we see a crowd of men in donkey jackets, including GARY, and two coaches. There is an OFFICIAL with a clipboard, who is calling out names.

Dad nervously walks up to them. He goes towards the official.

A BLOKE recognises Dad.

OFFICIAL
Is that the lot then?

BLOKE
Fuckin' hell. I never thought I'd see you down here.

OFFICIAL
Right, you, name?

DAD
Jackie Elliot.

OFFICIAL
Glad to see you've come to your senses.

GARY
Who's the big man now, eh?

Dad walks away and stands alone at the corner of the field and lights a rolly. He looks around at all the blokes. A cluster are laughing together but the whole thing has a sombre air.

OFFICIAL
Right. Okay, you lot, away. All aboard the skylark. Look lively.

Dad goes to get on the coach.

The coach drives away.

CUT TO:

INT. THE COACH — MORNING

The men are on their way to the pit. DAD is puffing on his rolly. A MINER accosts him.

MINER
Can't smoke on here, mate. These are private buses.

Dad throws his fag away.

CUT TO:

EXT. THE PICKET LINE — DAY

The picket line is in uproar as news of the impending arrival of the scab 'battlebus' filters through. The pickets try and block the road but are held back by the police.

CUT TO:

EXT. THE COACH — DAY

DAD stares ahead as the coach passes lines of police and reaches the pickets. The coach stops, lurches forward but is stopped by the pickets who have pushed the police into the road. The scabs begin to get worried as the pickets start rocking the coach from side to side. The grill on the back window gets pulled off. Missiles are thrown.

CUT TO:

EXT. THE PICKET LINE — THE SAME

TONY is yelling amongst other pickets on the other side of the road from Dad's seat.

EXT. THE COACH — THE SAME

DAD looks out at the mayhem to his left as a missile hits his window and the side grill is pulled away.

Dad moves over to the other side of the coach to avoid the faces of the pickets. As he sits he glances out of the window. He sees Tony shouting at the coach.

CUT TO:

EXT. THE PICKET LINE — THE SAME

TONY sees DAD. Tony stares in disbelief. His face is a picture of disbelief then anger. He pushes his way forward.

CUT TO:

EXT. THE COACH – THE SAME

DAD turns away. Through the window we see TONY fighting his way through the crowd until he reaches the window. He shouts:

Dad. Dad. What are you doing? Dad?

The coach pulls away and Tony is left speechless.

CUT TO:

EXT. THE PICKET LINE — THE SAME

TONY pushes his way through the crowd of pickets. He ducks through the police line and runs back towards the main road, pushing through police who try to stop him.

CUT TO:

EXT. THE COACH — THE SAME

The bus pulls up in a deserted part of the yard away from the pickets. The perimeter fence is nearby.

CUT TO:

EXT. THE PERIMETER FENCE — THE SAME

TONY is running at full pelt down the side of the perimeter fence after the bus.

CUT TO:

EXT. THE PERIMETER FENCE — THE SAME

TONY is standing alone holding on to the fence. He sees DAD.

TONY
Dad! What the fuck are you doing?

DAD
I don't know what else to do.

TONY
You can't go back. Not now.

DAD
Look at the state of us, man. What have we got to offer the poor sod?

TONY

You can't do this. Not now. Not after all this time. Not after everything we've been through.

DAD

It's for wee Billy.

TONY

Fuck!

DAD

He might be a fuckin' genius for all we know.

TONY

For fuck's sake, Dad, you can't do this, man. Dad. Dad.

A group of MINERS have followed Tony.

MINER I

Tony!

TONY

Dad, he's only eleven for fuck's sake. He's a kid.

DAD

I'm sorry. Sorry, son.

TONY

Dad. Dad. Please. Please.

DAD

I'm sorry, son. We're finished, son. What choice have we got, eh? Let's give the boy a fuckin' chance.

TONY

Please. Please, don't do this to me, Dad. We'll find him some money. We'll find it for him.

MINER I

What the fuck is he doing, Tony?

TONY

It's okay. He's gonna be okay.

MINER I

Away, leave it. Go on.

78

MINER 2

Just get him out of here, Tony.

MINER I

Come on.

CUT TO:

INT. ELLIOT HOUSE. BEDROOM — DARKNESS

BILLY and TONY lie in adjacent beds. Long pause.

TONY

Dad's right, you know. Mam would have let you.

CUT TO:

INT. HOUSE — LATER

BILLY has the table covered with piles of coins.

GEORGE

All them fifty pences. Here, it was a toss-up between a new
punch-bag or you.

TONY

It's not even enough for the bed and breakfast, man. Forget about it, you're dreaming. Look at youse. Fuckin' scrabbling around for fifty pences. You've gotta do better than that.

GEORGE

How, I'm gonna have a raffle at the welfare . . . and I'm gonna organise a concert.

BILLY

Thanks, George.

CUT TO:

INT. ELLIOT HOUSE. DAD'S BEDROOM — DAY

We see DAD looking at Mum's jewellery.

CUT TO:

EXT. PAWNSHOP — NEWCASTLE

DAD walks towards the pawnshop. He opens the door and goes in.

CUT TO:

EXT. STREET — DAY

DAD and BILLY walk down the road. Dad carries a suitcase. Billy dances.

DAD

Is that absolutely necessary? Walk normal, will you.

CUT TO:

INT. BUS. MOTORWAY — LATER

BILLY and DAD sit on the bus. Billy looks out at the motorway.

BILLY

So what's it like, like?

DAD

What's what like?

BILLY

London.

                           DAD

I don't know, son. I never made it past Durham.

                          BILLY

Have you never been, like?

                           DAD

Why would I want to go to London?

                          BILLY

Well, it's the Capital City.

                           DAD

Well, there's no mines in London.

                          BILLY

Christ, is that all you think about?

                                                    CUT TO:

EXT. MOTORWAY — AFTERNOON

*From outside the bus we see BILLY look out. The bus becomes a blur
as it races past us.*

                                                    CUT TO:

EXT. ROYAL BALLET SCHOOL — DAY

DAD and BILLY walk towards the school.

                                                    CUT TO:

INT. ENTRANCE TO ROYAL BALLET SCHOOL — DAY

A RECEPTIONIST is sitting at a desk. BILLY and DAD enter.

                      RECEPTIONIST

Can I help you?

                           DAD

Billy Elliot. We've come for an audition.

                      RECEPTIONIST

Oh, you mean William Elliot.

                           DAD

Yeah, William.

Ah yes. Can you go upstairs, please?

Dad glances at the stairs.

DAD
This way?

RECEPTIONIST
Yes.

DAD
Thanks.

They climb the stairs.

CUT TO:

INT. ROYAL BALLET SCHOOL. CHANGING ROOM — DAY

BILLY walks in past some other boys, SIMON and JOHN.

SIMON
This your first time?

JOHN
Yeah.

SIMON
Cor, I've been doing this for two years now.
                              (*to Billy*)
Hello. Nerve-racking isn't it? Where are you from?

BILLY
Everington. County Durham.

SIMON
Durham? Isn't there an amazing cathedral?

BILLY
Dunno. Never been.

CUT TO:

INT. ROYAL BALLET SCHOOL. MEDICAL ROOM — DAY

BILLY is measured by a TUTOR. A DOCTOR enters.

DOCTOR

Up on the box, please. Right, bend over. Right down and
come up. Up. Head UP. Tiny curvature here. Head down!
How tiny? Might not be a problem. Come on, keep coming.
Right. Right. Jump up, William.

BILLY

It's Billy. Billy Elliot.

CUT TO:

INT. ROYAL BALLET SCHOOL. HALL — LATER

DAD hangs round. He watches the LITTLE BALLERINAS dance.

*BILLY comes out in his dancing gear. He stands in the doorway. Dad
goes over to him.*

BILLY

Dad. Dad. Dad. For fuck's sake! I've changed me mind.

DAD

Get back in there! Don't be so stupid!

INT. ROYAL BALLET SCHOOL. AUDITION ROOM — LATER

*BILLY comes in. He looks over at a long desk behind which are
several TUTORS all looking solemn. We see in his body language that
he has lost all of his natural confidence. He looks small and vulnerable.*

TUTOR

And you are?

BILLY

Billy Elliot. From Everington.

TUTOR

I beg your pardon?

BILLY

Billy Elliot.

TUTOR

Ah yes, of course. Well then, come to the barre, please, Billy.

Billy walks to the barre.

Left arm on the barre. Feet first. Arms second. Demi-plié and hold.

CUT TO:

INT. HALL — THE SAME

DAD paces.

CUT TO:

INT. AUDITION ROOM — THE SAME

TUTOR

Now Billy, we'd like to see you move to some music. Do you have a piece prepared?

Music starts. BILLY stands there terrified. The music goes on. Billy still stands there. The music goes on and on Billy is just frozen. He feels his deepening crisis and humiliation. Finally . . .

Billy dances. He finishes. He is out of breath.

Mmm. Thank you.

INT. CHANGING ROOM — THE SAME

BILLY is in the changing room. He is in tears trying to contain himself. SIMON is in there on his own.

SIMON

Are you all right?

Billy ignores him and sits down.

SIMON

What's the matter?

BILLY

It was a waste of fuckin' time.

SIMON

Don't be upset. It's only a stupid audition.

Simon sits next to Billy, rather too close, to comfort him. Simon puts his arm around Billy. Billy shrugs him off. Simon comes back.

It's all right.

BILLY

Fuck off!

Simon tries to calm him.

SIMON

There's always next year.

BILLY

Look. Fuck off, will you.

Billy hits Simon and throws him viciously against the bench just as a WOMAN with a clipboard comes in.

BILLY

You bent bastard.

WOMAN

What on earth is going on here!

Billy looks at her in horror. Simon is lying across the benches – shocked and hurt.

CUT TO:

INT. ROYAL BALLET SCHOOL. WAITING ROOM – THE SAME

BILLY comes through looking like someone has died.

DAD

How did it go?

Billy goes off, his eyes full of tears.

DAD

Shit.

CUT TO:

INT. ROYAL BALLET SCHOOL. INTERVIEW ROOM – THE SAME

The panel of TUTORS are behind a long desk. BILLY and DAD are facing them nervously.

TUTOR

Mr. Elliot, I'm afraid that mutual respect and self-discipline are absolute pre-requisites of any pupil at this school. Such displays of violence cannot be tolerated under any circumstances. Do you understand?

Billy nods his head in embarrassment. Dad is equally embarrassed.

TUTOR 1

You realise that we shall have to consider this very seriously and it will be bound to affect our final decision. Yes, well, just a few questions then. Billy, could you tell us why you first became interested in ballet?

Long pause.

BILLY

Dunno.

Dad looks at him.

Just was.

TUTOR 1

Well, was there any specific aspect of ballet which caught your imagination?

Billy just stares.

BILLY

The dancing.

DAD

He dances all the time. Every night after school.

TUTOR 1

Yes, we have a very enthusiastic letter from Miss Wilkinson. She has told us of your personal circumstances.

TUTOR 1

Mr Elliot, are you a fan of the ballet?

DAD

I wouldn't exactly say I was an expert.

You do realise that pupils must attain the highest standards not just in ballet but also in their ordinary academic work. No child can succeed without the one hundred per cent support of his family. You are completely behind Billy? Are you not?

There is a pause before DAD answers.

DAD

Yes. Yes, of course.

The panel sense Dad's uncertainty.

TUTOR 2

Do you want to ask us any questions?

Dad looks blankly, then looks at Billy. Billy looks blank.

DAD

No. Not really.

TUTOR 1

Well, in that case, we shall let you know in due course.

Dad and Billy look devastated. It couldn't have gone worse, but just before they get up a WOMAN on the panel pipes up.

WOMAN

Just one last question. Can I just ask you, Billy, what does it feel like when you're dancing?

BILLY

Dunno. Sort of feels good. It's sort of stiff and that but once I get going then I like forget everything and, and sort of disappear. Sort of disappear – like I feel a change in me whole body – like there's fire in me whole body. I'm just there flying – like a bird. Like electricity. Yeah, like electricity.

Everyone has been stunned for a second by Billy's speech.

TUTOR 1

Have a safe journey home. And Mr Elliot, good luck with the strike.

INT. CORRIDOR — THE SAME

Dad and Billy walk down the corridor in silence.

INT. ELLIOT HOUSE. GRANDMA'S ROOM — DAY

DAD and BILLY sit on GRANDMA's bed.

GRANDMA

I think you should get yourself a trade, son. Something useful.

Dad gives Grandma a stern look.

GRANDMA

I could have been a professional dancer, you know.

Dad gives Grandma another withering stare.

INT./EXT. SCHOOL. CLASSROOM — MORNING.

BILLY is in the class. He is sitting next to MICHAEL. They are all listening to the teacher, who has a diagram of the earth on the board. She is explaining what coal is.

GIRL

So what happened to the dinosaurs, Miss?

TEACHER

They became crushed as well. And the pressure of all this caused the plants and trees to change into coal.

MICHAEL
(*to Billy*)

That must have been what happened to her.

BILLY

Shut up!

TEACHER

Michael Caffrey, if you have something to say you can say it to the whole class.

MICHAEL

Sorry, Miss.

TEACHER

So gradually over hundreds of thousands of years . . .

CUT TO:

INT. ELLIOT HOUSE. GRANDMA'S ROOM. DAY

GRANDMA stares through the window. She sees the postman clutching letters.

GRANDMA

Post!

CUT TO:

INT. ELLIOT HOUSE. HALL – SAME

DAD enters and takes the letter from the letterbox. He looks at it.

DAD

This is it.

CUT TO:

EXT. STREET – THE SAME

BILLY is walking home. He bumps into GEORGE.

GEORGE

Have you heard anything yet?

BILLY

Not yet.

GEORGE

You'll have no problem. Fingers crossed, eh?

Billy smiles, but as he turns away we see the look of anxiety on his face.

INT. ELLIOT HOUSE — LATER

CLOSE UP of the letter on the table. TONY is there too, looking stern. In the background, we hear the door open. BILLY comes into the room and looks at DAD, who looks at the letter. Billy stands still, struck dumb with nervousness. Everyone waits with anticipation. The process is long-drawn-out and extremely nerve-racking.

Billy tentatively goes over to the letter. Picks it up and goes into GRANDMA's room. He sits down and opens it. And starts to read it to himself. Billy's face is, however, immobile. Then very slowly his hands shake and he breaks into silent tears.

Dad and Tony wait outside. The tension is too much. They run into Grandma's room. They see the shock on Billy's face. Dad and Tony are almost at breaking-point. Billy looks up.

                    BILLY
     I got in.

                                        CUT TO:

INT. STREET — DAY

DAD running at full pelt down the street.

                                        CUT TO:

INT. SOCIAL CLUB — THE SAME

The door bursts open. DAD runs in. He sees GEORGE et al. in the corner. Dad shouts, breathlessly:

                    DAD
     He did it. He fucking did it.

No reaction. Dad is taken aback by this singular lack of enthusiasm.

                    MINER 1
     Jackie? Have you not heard, man. We're going back.

                    MINER 2
     It's over, Jackie.

MINER 3

We lost. Back to work on Monday.

EXT. GRAVEYARD — DAY

BILLY is sitting by his Mum's grave with DAD.

BILLY

I think I'm scared, Dad.

They stare at each other.

DAD

That's okay, son. We're all scared.

BILLY

Well, if I don't like it, can I still come back?

DAD

Are you kidding? We've let out your room.

Billy smiles. Dad smiles back. They burst into laughter.

CUT TO:

INT. BOXING HALL — DAY

BILLY is waiting for MRS. WILKINSON. She is teaching the girls. We hear her shouting her instructions.

BILLY

Miss, I just came to tell you.

MRS. WILKINSON

It's all right, Billy, I heard it from Debbie.

BILLY

Look, it was just, well you know, after everything.

Mrs. Wilkinson allows some space.

BILLY

I'll miss you, Miss.

MRS. WILKINSON

No you won't.

BILLY

I will, honest.

MRS. WILKINSON

This is when you go out and find life and all those other
things. The best of luck, Billy.

*That's it. Billy looks at her. She turns and goes back to the class. Billy
turns and walks away.*

CUT TO:

INT. ELLIOT HOUSE. KITCHEN — DAY

*DAD and TONY are waiting for BILLY with coats on. Billy runs in
from seeing Mrs. Wilkinson. GRANDMA sits at the table.*

DAD

Was she there?

BILLY

Yeah.

TONY

You'll miss the bus.

DAD

We're off.

Tony turns to pick up the suitcase.

BILLY

I'll take it.

*Dad and Tony walk out. Billy goes to Grandma. She leaps up and
hugs him.*

CUT TO:

EXT. BACK YARD — THE SAME

*BILLY struggles up the steps with his case. DAD and TONY help.
Billy looks up at Michael's house opposite. No sign of Michael, only
the SNOTTY LITTLE GIRL who is always in the lane.*

SNOTTY LITTLE GIRL

Goodbye, Billy.

BILLY

See you.

CUT TO:

EXT. BACK LANE — THE SAME

The trio walk down the hill. We see MICHAEL climb onto his coal shed. As BILLY, TONY and DAD reach the end of the lane, Michael yells.

MICHAEL

Oi. Dancing boy.

Billy runs back.

DAD

We'll miss the bus.

TONY

Will you stop being an old fucking woman.

Billy places his hands on Michael's shoulders, pulls him close and kisses his cheek.

BILLY

See you, then.

He smiles and runs off.

CUT TO:

EXT. BUS STATION — LATER

DAD hugs BILLY.

Billy climbs onto the bus.

Billy watches Dad leave the bus and looks out the window at Tony. Tony mouths something that Billy cannot hear or understand.

BILLY

What? What?

Tony is obviously saying it much louder now.

What? I can't hear you.

The bus pulls off. TONY outside the bus shouting:

TONY

    I'll miss you.

Billy runs to the back of the bus as it drives off.

CUT TO:

INT. PIT. CAGE — THE SAME

All the MINERS stand in the cage ready to be taken down to work. They stand tightly packed. The lift door shuts and the lift descends plunging all the faces into darkness.

CUT TO:

INT. MRS. WILKINSON'S DANCING SCHOOL — DAY

Ballet class. MRS. WILKINSON is doing her 'UP, two, three, four'.

CUT TO:

INT. COACH. DAY.

BILLY is looking out of the window going down the motorway to London.

CUT TO:

EXT. LONDON — DAY

A modern-day tube train draws up. Out get an older DAD and TONY. Dad wanders in the wrong direction.

TONY

    Dad. Come on, man. We're gonna be late.

They exit up the escalators.

CUT TO:

EXT. THE THEATRE ROYAL — THE SAME

DAD and TONY walk up to the front door.

The DOORMAN intercepts them.

DOORMAN

It's just started.

CUT TO:

INT. AUDITORIUM — EVENING

DAD and TONY are ushered to their seats.

DAD

Excuse me . . . can you tell Billy Elliot that his family's here?
Okay?

*Tony accidentally bumps the young man next to him. He does not
recognise MICHAEL.*

TONY

Sorry, mate.

MICHAEL

It's all right, Tony.

Tony is amazed.

MICHAEL

It's me. Michael. Remember?

TONY
(*to Dad*)

It's Michael.

TONY

What the bloody hell are you doing here?

MICHAEL

I wouldn't have missed it for the world.

CUT TO:

INT. SIDE OF STAGE — THE SAME

*The music increasing in tension. BILLY, now in his early twenties, is
looking on to the stage. We don't see his face but see the back of his
head as the music is playing loudly in his ears. We feel his heart beating
fast. The music wells up still further.*

96

INT. AUDITORIUM – THE SAME

CLOSE UP of DAD and TONY. BALLERINAS are on stage. 'Swan Lake'. The music increasing in tension – yet again.

CUT TO:

INT. SIDE OF STAGE – THE SAME

The music gets louder and louder. The anticipation cannot get any higher. BILLY's heart pounding. He leaps onto the stage. Silence. As if we are inside Billy's skull. The bright lights seem blinding.

Then a cranking guitar suddenly strikes in and the music accompanying Billy's dance is not 'Swan Lake', but 'Ride a White Swan' by T. Rex.

SONG
'Riding on out like a bird in a sky race, / Riding on out like you were a bird.'